United States Army

RICHARD BARTLETT

Heinemann Library
Chicago, Illinois

Designed by Herman Adler Design
Photo research by Bill Broyles
Printed and bound in the United States by Lake Book
Manufacturing Inc.

08 07 06 05 04
10 9 8 7 6 5 4 3 2 1

Library of Congress Cataloging-in-Publication Data

Bartlett, Richard.
  Know it! United States Army / by Richard Bartlett.
    p. cm.
  Summary: Provides an overview of the United States Army,
including its history, weapons, and vehicles.
  Includes bibliographical references and index.
    ISBN 1-40340-188-8 (Hardcover) -- ISBN 1-40340-445-3
(Paperback)
  1. United States. Army--Juvenile literature. [1. United
States. Army.] I. Title.
  UA25 .B26 2003
  355'.00973--dc21
                                        2002015483

Acknowledgments
The author and publisher are grateful to the following for
permission to reproduce copyright material:
Cover photograph by Mark Gibson/Index Stock Imagery
Title page, pp. 5, 8, 13, 14B, 17, 22, 24T, 26, 27, 29T, 30,
33T, 42L, 43B, 45R Department of Defense; pp. 4, 42R
United States Army; pp. 6, 33B Corbis; p. 7 Paul J.
Richards/AFP/Getty Images; pp. 9, 18, 19, 28 Leif
Skoogfors/Corbis; p. 10 Medford Historical Society
Collection/Corbis; p. 11B Reuters NewMedia Inc./Corbis;
p. 11T Jim Mone/AP Wide World Photo; p. 12 Burstein
Collection/Corbis; pp. 14T, 21B, 38, 39 Bettmann/Corbis;
p. 15 Rodger Mallison/AP Wide World Photo; pp. 16, 31
Romeo Gacad/AFP/Getty Images; p. 20 Rudi von
Briel/Heinemann Library; p. 21T The Robert N. Dennis
Collection of Stereoscopic Views NYPG91-F168 054F/New
York Public Library; p. 23 Laffont Jean Pierre/Corbis
SYGMA; p. 24B MD Helicopters; pp. 25L, 25R, 44L, 45L,
45C U.S. Army Institute of Heraldry; p. 25C H. J. Saunders
U.S. Military Insignia, Inc.; p. 29B Dan
Chung/Reuters/Corbis; p. 32 United States Air Force; p. 34
Library of Congress; p. 35 U.S. Army Quartermaster
Museum; p. 36T Joseph Sohm/ChromoSohm Inc./Corbis;
p. 36B Margaret Bourke-White/Time Life Pictures/Getty
Images; p. 37 Wally McNamee/Corbis; p. 40 Hulton
Archive/Getty Images; p. 41 Richard Cummins/Corbis;
p. 43T Sikorsky Aircraft Corporation; p. 44R Congressional
Medal of Honor Society

Special thanks to Lt. Col. G.A. Lofaro for his review of
this book.

Every effort has been made to contact copyright holders
of any material reproduced in this book. Any omissions
will be rectified in subsequent printings if notice is given
to the publisher.

Note to the Reader: Some words are shown in
bold, **like this.** You can find out what they mean
by looking in the glossary.

Contents

The Army Spirit

Can you imagine risking your life for someone you have never met? The men and women of the United States Army take such risks every day. For more than 200 years, this willingness to risk danger has been part of the job for the men and women who have worn the uniform of the U.S. Army.

The U.S. Army has fought in forests and deserts, on mountains and islands. Soldiers have sometimes been cold or hot, hungry, and homesick. But they always perform their jobs with bravery and pride. Their duties include not only fighting, but also **humanitarian** peacekeeping missions.

The U.S. Army and its people are always on the alert for danger.

The official army emblem has the motto "This we'll defend" above a red cap. The cap dates back to Roman times. These caps were worn by slaves during the ceremony at which they were set free. It is often called the liberty cap. So, the motto means that the U.S. Army will defend liberty, which is another word for freedom. The cap has been used as a symbol of liberty in this country since 1765.

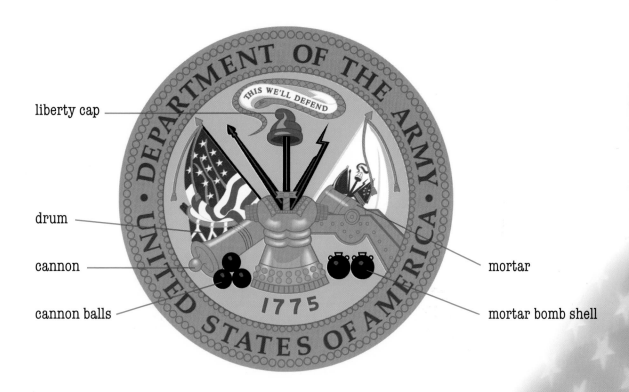

liberty cap

drum

cannon

cannon balls

mortar

mortar bomb shell

For many years, the army emblem was used only on documents. It was not displayed in public. In 1974, the secretary of the army approved this version as the official symbol of the U.S. Army.

What is the U.S. Army?

The U.S. Army is one of several military forces. Other military forces are the marines, the navy, and the air force. The army is the oldest military force. It was first organized during the Revolutionary War in 1775. Army **personnel** are mostly responsible for fighting on land. However, to reach their battle sites and support ground troops, they often use airplanes, helicopters, and boats.

How was the army formed?

During the Revolutionary War, all members of the army were volunteers. The men were offered money and free land when the war was over. In the 1860s, the country was fighting the Civil War. Confederate army volunteers only had to serve for one year. Union soldiers enlisted for three or nine months. The war was taking longer to win than anyone thought it would. Many men were losing their lives in battle and from sickness. Both armies needed more people. Each side passed a conscription law, or a **draft** law. This law ordered men to register with their government. They had to serve in the army if they were needed.

The army has some unusual ways of getting onto the ground, where they do their fighting.

The United States maintained a draft law, called a Selective Service Act, through World Wars I and II, the Korean War, and the Vietnam War. In 1973 the Act was no longer in effect, and men did not have to register for the draft. In 1980, the U.S. Congress reinstituted draft registration. However, it only permitted the government to register the men. They could not be put into the army unless another law was passed by Congress. Today, all male citizens between the ages of 18 and 26 must register, but the act does not allow them to be drafted into the army without permission from Congress. So, everyone that you see in the army today is a volunteer.

Know It

Even though women can serve in the Army, they do not have to register. They cannot be drafted.

In July 2001 David Edmond Lucitt (right) became the one millionth man to register on-line for the U.S. Selective Service.

Registration Acknowledgement Card   SSS Form 3A (03-01)

SELECTIVE SERVICE NUMBER   DATE OF BIRTH   SOCIAL SECURITY NUMBER   LAST ACTION DATE
▼ 83-0426250-7   ▼ 06-10-83   ▼ XXX-XX-XXXX   06-11-01

The Selective Service System thanks you for registering. This form is your official Registration Acknowledgement Card. Tear it out and safeguard it as your proof of having registered.

NAME AND CURRENT ADDRESS

▼ DAVID EDMOND LUCITT   DIRECTOR

HAYMARKET, VA 20169   ▼

▲ SIGNATURE OF REGISTRANT

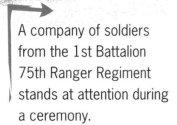

A company of soldiers from the 1st Battalion 75th Ranger Regiment stands at attention during a ceremony.

There are three types of **personnel** in the U.S. Army. **Active-duty** members work at their army jobs full time. The other two types of soldiers are National Guardsmen and Army Reservists. These soldiers are part-time soldiers. They are stationed close to their homes and work one weekend every month and two full weeks during the year.

All soldiers are either enlisted men and women, warrant officers, or **commissioned** officers. There are five ways to become an officer. The Reserve Officer Training Corps (ROTC) allows college students to take regular classes and train to be officers at the same time. Officer Candidate School (OCS) is open to enlisted soldiers and warrant officers. These soldiers attend OCS for about three months. Then they become commissioned officers.

The United States Military Academy is a military college in New York. All graduates are commissioned as second lieutenants. Some people join the army and receive direct **commissions.** These men and women, such as doctors and lawyers, already have college degrees and training in special fields.

Finally, during wartime, some soldiers receive battlefield commissions. These soldiers have demonstrated that they have the ability to lead soldiers in combat.

Know It

The cavalry has been one kind of army unit since the Revolutionary War. Horses were used for transport as late as 1957. Today, the soldiers of the army's First Cavalry Division still ride into battle. Now, they use tanks, helicopters, and armored personnel carriers.

One field army could have as many as 400,000 people.

1 corps = 5 divisions =
    5 x 16,000 = 80,000 people
1 Field army = 5 corps =
    5 x 80,000 = 400,000 people

When the U.S. Army goes into combat, army personnel are organized into the groups shown in the diagram. Within each of these groups, people have different jobs. These include operating tanks, **artillery,** helicopters, and communications equipment. Some personnel are the traditional foot soldiers. Foot soldiers are called the **infantry.**

Field Army
Contains 2 to 5 Corps

Corps
Contains 2 to 5 Divisions

Division
Contains 10,000 to 16,000 people

Brigade
Contains 3,000 to 5,000 people

Battalion
Contains 500 to 900 people

Company
Contains 90 to 200 people

The 1st Armored Division was stationed in Germany after World War II. In 1994, after its final review shown here, the unit returned to the United States.

Armies Through the Years

When the Declaration of Independence was signed in 1776, there was no National Guard or any type of national army. Instead, each town had a local **militia** that had been formed to protect settlers. These militias were made up of **civilian** volunteers who were willing to take up arms whenever their neighbors and communities were threatened. For the settlers, the militia became important to their security. This made it possible for people to start settlements in the colonies.

The role of the militia expanded when the colonies became a nation. Each state was to have a militia that could be called to fight for the new United States. Today's Army National Guard has taken the place of the state militias.

During peacetime, these soldiers can be ordered to carry out different kinds of missions, ranging from crowd control to capturing escaped prisoners. They also provide much needed help during local disasters such as floods, earthquakes, and forest fires.

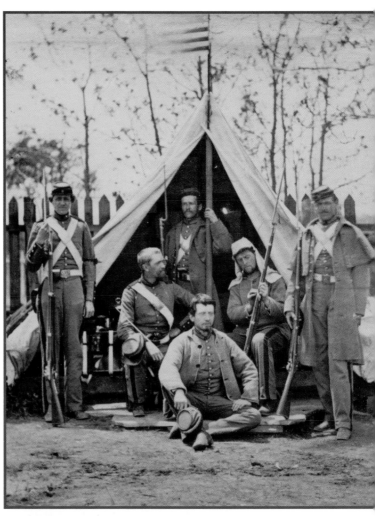

These soldiers were photographed in 1861 during the Civil War.

Following the terrorist attacks on New York and Washington, D.C., the president of the United States ordered several thousand soldiers of the Army National Guard to **active duty.** They were asked to join in the fight against terrorism. Many fought in the deserts of Afghanistan. Others were asked to stay behind and protect their homeland from further attacks.

National Guardsmen in Minnesota were called to help during a flood in 1997.

In November 2001, a National Guardsman patrolled Miami International Airport in Florida.

This painting shows soldiers during the Revolutionary War (1775–1783). Notice that not all of the soldiers have uniforms. Some soldiers even had to bring their own guns.

Armies of the 1700s

In the 1700s fighting **tactics** were rather simple. Most soldiers were **infantry.** These men stood in long straight lines when they fought. However, even at that time there were some men who used what we now call **unconventional** warfare tactics. They did not march in **formation** like other soldiers. They moved in secret through the woods and fought in small groups.

Armies of the 1800s

In the 1800s, the United States fought the War of 1812, the Mexican War, and the Civil War. The armies were larger, and cannons and other **artillery** played a more important part in battles. But the range of the artillery was short, and soldiers still had to get fairly close to the enemy before the fighting could begin. During the Civil War, infantry and cavalry divisions were formed. These developments meant that more soldiers were needed to take care of the equipment and horses and to transport supplies.

The Third Cavalry proudly carried its flags in Cuba in 1898.

Modern armies

The U.S. Army of the early 1900s was much like the Civil War army. Officers still rode on horseback while most troops moved from place to place on foot. By the time World War I ended in 1918, things had started to change. The army had started to become **mechanized.** Over time, jeeps and trucks were used in place of horses.

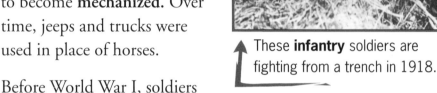

These **infantry** soldiers are fighting from a trench in 1918.

Before World War I, soldiers usually fought standing up, out in the open. During World War I, soldiers dug miles of **trenches** along the **front lines.** Often, these trenches were so close that each side could talk to the other. The soldiers would shoot at each other from the trenches. After World War I, tanks and **artillery** did much of the heavy fighting. Communication radios let officers direct battles from greater distances than ever before. Modern **technology** had come to the U.S. Army.

During World War II, the U.S. Army used large forces of infantry, tanks, artillery, ships, and other equipment to transport troops and carry out the fighting. This is Italy, 1943.

During World War I, automatic weapons replaced many single-shot rifles. In World War II, automatic weapons were greatly improved. Tanks were also faster and more powerful. By the end of World War II, the army had used more than 57,000 tanks, 476,000 rocket launchers, 1,000 8-inch (200-millimeter) howitzers, and 4 billion rounds of ammunition to defeat the enemy.

In the years following World War II, the U.S. Army continued to develop its technology. New materials for building weapons and clothing soldiers, computers, and satellites all combined to make the U.S. Army the most advanced in the world.

An army captain checks a computer map while inside his Humvee.

Army People

Enlisted personnel

The first rank in the army is the private. The private rank (also called an E-1) is the lowest rank in the army. There are nine ranks for **enlisted personnel.** After two more private ranks (E-2 and E3), the next rank is the corporal or specialist. Corporals and higher ranks are **noncommissioned officers** (NCOs).

The man without a helmet is a sergeant. The man on the right is a corporal. They are watching a private first class (on the left) as he works a machine gun.

Corporals and sergeants are NCOs. They are in charge of the corporals and privates ranked below them. Sergeants help with training of individuals and must be good leaders. Each of the next sergeant ranks has more and more responsibilities for larger numbers of people and equipment. A sergeant first class, the seventh highest enlisted rank, usually has fifteen to eighteen years of experience. The top enlisted position in the army is sergeant major of the army. This rank was established in 1966.

Warrant officers

Warrant officers are enlisted personnel who have gone through special training. They rank higher than enlisted personnel. More than 12,000 warrant officers are on **active duty.** They work in all areas of the army, including special operations forces, good service, criminal investigations, **intelligence,** and even the military band.

General John Shalikashvili (left), now retired, was the chairman of the Joint Chiefs of Staff when he met with these soldiers in 1993.

Commissioned officers

There are ten ranks of **commissioned** officers. These are people who have attended the United States Military Academy at West Point, Officer Candidate School (OCS), or the Army Reserve Officer Training Corps (ROTC). Commissioned officers have specialties that include combat, communications, finance, and personnel management.

The Generals' bosses

The head of the army is the commander in chief, who is also the president of the United States. The commander in chief is the head of all the military branches—the army, the navy, the air force, and the marine corps. Under the commander in chief is the secretary of defense, who is a member of the president's **cabinet.** This person gives advice and makes decisions about how the U.S. military should operate. Below the secretary of defense are the Joint Chiefs of Staff, which include the highest officers from each branch of the military. They advise the president and the secretary of defense.

Know It

Each type of general wears a different number of stars on his or her uniform. A brigadier general has one star, a major general has two, lieutenant generals have three, generals have four, and generals of the army have five stars.

Basic Training

Most men and women in the army are **enlisted personnel.** These new army personnel, called recruits, must go through a nine-week basic training course. But before recruits enter basic training, they are sent to a Reception Battalion for two or three weeks.

While in the Reception Battalion, recruits get identification cards and their first military haircuts—"high and tight" for the men (very, very short) and short hair for the women (ponytails are not allowed). They are given sweatsuits to wear for the first several days. Uniforms are issued later. They receive eye and dental exams and take their Physical Assessment Test. If they do not pass, they must attend a special camp to improve their physical condition before they are sent to basic training. Reception is where recruits learn how to take care of their **barracks** and march in **formation.**

A female recruit performs a physical fitness test during basic training.

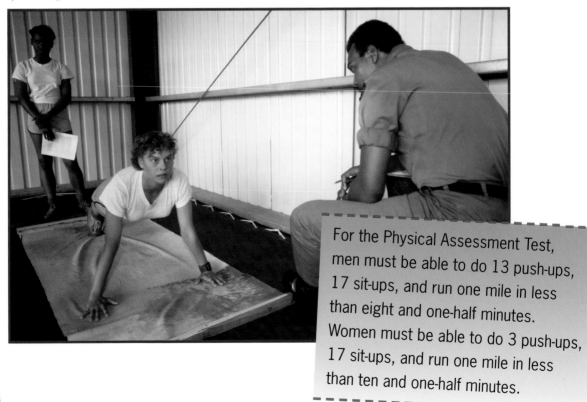

For the Physical Assessment Test, men must be able to do 13 push-ups, 17 sit-ups, and run one mile in less than eight and one-half minutes. Women must be able to do 3 push-ups, 17 sit-ups, and run one mile in less than ten and one-half minutes.

This recruit is learning how to use a bayonet by stabbing a tire.

Boot camp

At the end of Reception, recruits ship out to another location for basic training. Now their physical conditioning drills become harder. They must learn the military skills necessary for all soldiers. Recruits will pair off to learn hand-to-hand combat. As a group, they will practice **guerrilla** warfare exercises, study military **tactics,** and learn about weapons. The standard rifle issued in the army is the M-16A2. Recruits learn how to shoot it and also how to take it apart and put it back together so that it can be cleaned.

These new soldiers must learn how to camp the army way, with army equipment. They will learn how to **camouflage** themselves and their camps. Because soldiers sometimes find themselves under attack when they do not expect it, they must learn how to quickly take cover and set up defensive positions. And because of the dangers of combat, all soldiers must learn first aid.

Military Tradition: Officer Training at West Point

To educate, train, and inspire the Corps of Cadets so that each graduate is a commissioned leader of character committed to the values of Duty, Honor, Country; professional growth throughout a career as an officer in the United States Army, and a lifetime of selfless service to the nation.

These words describe the purpose of the U.S. Military Academy at West Point. It is here that many future army officers receive the training and skills that will prepare them to be leaders, during peace and in times of war. Located 50 miles (80 kilometers) north of New York City, the Academy celebrated its 200th anniversary in 2002.

↑ A West Point color guard marching in formation.

The importance of West Point as a military training facility is seen in the names of some of its most famous graduates. Robert E. Lee and Ulysses S. Grant from the Civil War were both Academy graduates. President of the United States Dwight D. Eisenhower was the Supreme Commander of **Allied** Forces in Europe during World War II. Other great names include Douglas MacArthur and George Patton. Kristin Baker, a 1990 graduate, is also famous. She was the first woman

Leading the battle

For 55 of the 60 battles fought during the Civil War, both the North and the South were led by West Point graduates. For the other battles, at least one side was led by a West Point man.

In the 1870s, two cadets posed with a little girl visiting their training exercise. The cadet on the right has traded his cap for the girl's bonnet.

to be named Brigade Commander of the Academy's student body, known as the Corps of **Cadets.**

Good grades are important to gain admission to West Point. The Academy also wants people who can best meet the physical and mental challenges faced by every officer in the U.S. Army. In addition, West Point works to include a mix of top scholars, athletes, women, and **minorities.** This helps to increase understanding and tolerance among the 4,000 cadets who attend the Academy every year.

Know It

Learning to be an effective officer requires more than learning about weapons and how to plan a battle. At West Point, cadets take classes in military science (battle **tactics**), history, economics, math, literature, political science, and law.

When cadets graduate, they receive a bachelor of science degree and a **commission** in the U.S. Army. After serving a minimum of five years on **active duty,** they may choose to continue their careers in the military or go on to work as **civilians.**

In 1976, West Point admitted its first women cadets. Out of a class of 1,485, there were 105 women.

Invisible Warriors: Army Special Operations

The officers that graduate from West Point and the people they command are the army that is usually seen by the American public. But there are many other soldiers who work quietly, often in secret. These are the soldiers of the U.S. Army Special Operations Command. Those who volunteer for special operations undergo training that is so demanding that only a few complete the training.

Rangers

Army Rangers have a history that goes back to the French and Indian War, fought in the mid-1700s. They moved quickly and quietly through the woods and swamps to fight the enemy. In the wars that followed, Rangers developed ways to fulfill their mission to "hit hard, hit fast, and then get out so larger and more heavily armed groups could move in and complete the job."

These Army Rangers are practicing their attack **tactics**.

Today, Rangers are airborne troops that are often the first to face the enemy. They are trained to strike enemy targets such as airfields, either by landing in aircraft or by parachuting. The Rangers' skills allow them to enter rough terrain, such as mountains, and surprise the enemy.

Green Berets conduct a training exercise in guerrilla warfare for foreign soldiers.

Special Forces

Special Forces, also called Green Berets, are highly skilled at a special kind of warfare, called **guerrilla** warfare. They are often assigned to train foreign troops and to gather **intelligence,** or information about the enemy. Unlike the Rangers, Green Berets may have missions that require them to stay in enemy territory for a long time, perhaps months. They need to speak the language of the area they are in. They need to understand the culture and blend in with the local people. Sometimes they work in civilian clothes. Green Berets must already be experienced soldiers when they volunteer. They must already have at least a sergeant's rank. Many Rangers move on to be Green Berets.

The basic Special Forces unit has only twelve men. Special Forces was established in 1952. They wore green berets because they felt that the work they did was so different from **conventional** warfare, that they deserved a special hat. In 1961, with President John Kennedy's support, it became the official hat of the Special Forces.

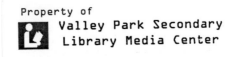

↑ An MH-47 Chinook flies at sunset.

SOAR through the skies

The members of the 160th Special Operations Aviation Regiment, or SOAR, are known as Night Stalkers. Their main responsibility is to provide air support to the special operations forces on the ground. The nickname comes from being highly skilled at night flying. Night Stalkers fly many kinds of aircraft including heavy assault helicopters and small, fast-attack helicopters known as Little Birds.

The first SOAR unit was officially established in 1981. In 1990 it became part of the U.S. Army Special Operations Command. The men assigned to SOAR are some of the best pilots and soldiers. Both officers and **enlisted** men can join.

This is the Little Bird helicopter. It's just big enough for two soldiers.

Delta Force

Noncommissioned officers, warrant officers, and **commissioned** officers who are looking for a special challenge can volunteer for Delta Force. No one knows how many men are in Delta Force or what their missions are. Even the training they go through is secret. Their training camp is off limits even to most other army **personnel.** We do know that they were formed in 1977 to fight terrorism overseas, rescue hostages, and conduct **reconnaissance.** Members of Delta Force work in small strike teams. They are considered among the finest combat troops in the world. There are no photographs of Delta Force. They are so secret that the government does not talk about what they do or how they train.

Army 75th Rangers Regime

Special Forces Airborne

Army Special Operations

Army People without Guns

Not everyone in the army uses a gun or drives a tank to perform military duties. There are hundreds of jobs that must be done to support the soldiers who fight in the battlefield. Supplies must be ordered and delivered. Equipment must be cared for. People must receive their paychecks. Buildings must be built. The injured and sick must be treated. All of these things must be done in peacetime and during war. Once they complete their basic training, **enlisted personnel** can choose from hundreds of different jobs. Here is information about some of them.

Combat documentation/production specialist

The army documents many combat and noncombat operations through videos and photographs. Movies are also used to train personnel. Combat documentation/production specialists help prepare the scripts, plan the filming, and operate and maintain the recording equipment. These people train from 7 to 52 weeks to learn the skills for this job. After their army service, they may choose careers as motion-picture camera operators or broadcast and recording technicians.

An army specialist repairs a video camera in the Fort Sam Houston Audio/Visual Production Facility in Fort Sam Houston, San Antonio, Texas.

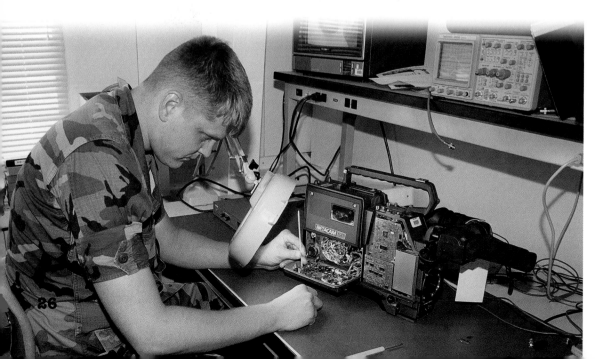

Administrative specialist

Administrative specialists record, store, and deliver information necessary to plan and direct army operations. Duties include typing letters and reports, organizing files, scheduling training for personnel, and answering phones. The training involves six to ten weeks of classroom instruction. This work prepares the soldier for civilian jobs as secretaries and administrative assistants.

Finance specialist

After six to twelve weeks of classroom instruction, finance specialists are ready to perform their assigned job. They are responsible for organizing and keeping track of army records that detail how much money is being spent and where it is being spent. These men and women may have an interest in mathematics and accounting. When they have completed their army duty, they will be qualified to work as **civilian** bookkeepers and accountants.

Multimedia illustrator

The army's training manuals, newspapers, reports, signs, charts, and posters all require pictures, or graphics. Multimedia illustrators create these graphics. They must operate and maintain the equipment needed in their job. The graphics might be used to show numbers of troops and supplies. Or they might create illustrations of the human body for medical training. These skills help the soldiers find jobs in advertising, web design, or print shops when their military service is over.

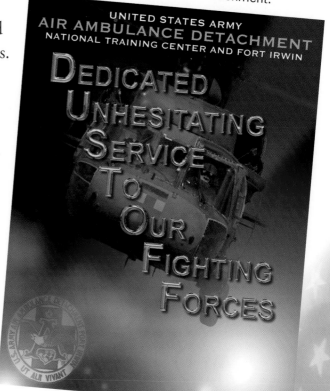

This poster informs people about the U.S. Army Air Ambulance Detachment.

Radio operator/maintainer

The army requires a lot of communications equipment to track and direct the movements of troops, group equipment, aircraft, and ships. Radios are one type of equipment that is used. Radio operator/ maintainers test and repair the radios, install equipment, prepare and send messages, and receive messages. These positions require 8 to 40 weeks of training after basic training. Men and women who perform this job may have careers as radio mechanics after their army service.

Satellite communications systems operator/maintainer

Sometimes the army uses more complicated communications equipment than radios. Satellites are an important part of today's army operations. Equipment on the ground is needed to receive information from satellites. Satellite communications systems operators/maintainers use this equipment to send and receive messages through satellites. They also install and repair the equipment. These skills prepare them for **civilian** jobs with airports, telephone companies, and police and fire departments.

These soldiers are setting up satellite communications equipment. This type of equipment helps soldiers in the field complete their missions safely.

A D7E Earthmover is one type of vehicle that Heavy Construction Equipment Operators must learn to use.

Heavy construction equipment operator

Whether the army is building bases in the United States or setting up temporary bases in other countries, tons of building materials must be moved and put into place. In many cases, roads and airfield landing strips must be built. Heavy construction equipment operators are needed to drive bulldozers, roadgraders, and tractor-trailers that carry construction equipment.

It takes four to twelve weeks of training to get ready to do this kind of job. But the skills learned are useful for many civilian careers, including working for building contractors and being a heavy equipment operator.

Diver

Army divers are needed to perform repairs, inspections of ships, **reconnaissance,** and demolition that must be done underwater. They also salvage, or save, equipment that has sunk. Scuba divers work just below the surface. They use metal tanks that supply air to breathe underwater. Other divers are trained as deep sea divers and stay under the water for long periods of time at depths up to 300 feet (91 meters).

These skills may prepare them for jobs with oil companies and underwater construction companies. Former army divers might also work for police and fire rescue services.

Army divers must have the skills to work in unusual places.These army divers and chemical weapons experts are inspecting a base in Iraq that was used by a member of Saddam Hussein's government. They are looking for chemical weapons.

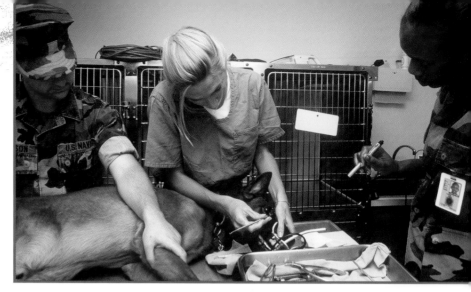

Max, an army dog, gets his teeth cleaned by a dental technician second class, while his trainer (left) stands by.

Animal care specialist

The army has patrol dogs, horses (used in ceremonies), and even sled dogs that are used in arctic rescue missions. The animal care specialist is supervised by a veterinary corps officer. He or she takes care of army animals. This includes keeping them well fed and clean and treating them for illness and injury when necessary. After basic training, animal care specialists spend 7 to 52 weeks in additional training.

Operating room specialist

Operating room specialists help the nurses prepare patients and operating rooms for surgery. They can also begin treatment of patients when the army doctors are busy, especially under battlefield conditions. Their duties can include cleaning the operating room, recording the patient's medical history, taking a patient's temperature and blood pressure, giving shots, and performing basic emergency medical care. These skills can be applied later to careers in **civilian** hospitals.

With all of the advanced equipment, you would never know that this operating room nurse is on duty in the field in Africa.

Helicopter repairer

All army fighting vehicles need to be maintained and repaired. Each type of vehicle requires special training to understand how it works and how to fix it. AH-64 attack helicopter repairers only work on the AH-64 attack helicopters, also know as Apache helicopters.

These people must be able to fix just about anything on the Apache, including its engines, fuel and electric systems, and landing gear. When his or her military service is completed, an AH-64 attack helicopter repairer might move on to a career with commercial airlines or companies that build aircraft.

These U.S. Army air mechanics are replacing a Blackhawk helicopter's power unit while on duty in Iraq in 2003.

Military police

The army has its own law enforcement and security **personnel** to handle crime on army property. The military police also control traffic and respond to emergencies. They may patrol on foot or in cars or boats. Their eight to twelve weeks of training includes classes on military and civilian laws, investigation procedures, and evidence collection. This job provides a good background for a later career in **civilian** law enforcement.

A member of the U.S. Army's 101st Military Police Company gives a child some food in Afghanistan. Public relations can be as important as enforcing the law.

Special band member

The military has a long tradition of performing at ceremonies, parades, and concerts. A special band member performs with the U.S. Army Band, the U.S. Army Field Band, the U.S. Military Academy Band, or the 3rd **Infantry** (Old Guard) Fife and Drum Corps.

The modern version of the Fife and Drum Corps marches during a parade in Washington, D.C.

However, even these musicians must go through basic training and learn how to be a soldier, including how to shoot a rifle. In times of war, all trained soldiers may be called upon to fight.

Cryptologic linguist

Cryptography is secret writing or codes. Cryptologic means having to do with codes. A linguist is someone who knows a lot about languages . The army's cryptologic linguists use special equipment to find foreign communications. They identify the language being used and translate the messages into English. They also read newspapers and other materials in foreign languages. They look for certain words that may be codes carrying information. Some cryptologic linguists train for as long as a year after their basic training. They can go on as civilians to careers as translators for universities, businesses, and even the government.

This painting, created around 1876, shows fife and drum players during the Revolutionary War in 1776.

33

Army Animals and The Quartermaster Corps

Early armies needed animals just as today's armies need tanks, trucks, and helicopters. Riding horses was the only way for many soldiers to get to the battlefield. Officers rode horses to move between the units they were directing in battle. They sometimes fought on horseback with swords. Horses and mules pulled supply wagons. Later, horses pulled the **artillery.**

Finding, buying, and handing out supplies to the army is the job of the Army Quartermaster Corps. The first Quartermaster General position was established in 1775. In later years, other Quartermaster Departments were set up to provide food and clothing for the troops, pay soldiers, bury the dead, and take care of national cemeteries. In 1912, all the departments were combined into the Quartermaster Corps, which still exists.

In 1864, these Quartermaster soldiers took a break from distributing supplies.

The Quartermaster Corps is often the first to be sent to an area where military operations will take place. Quartermaster soldiers must move in supplies and prepare for the thousands of troops that will be **deployed.** Quartermaster soldiers have been dog trainers, bakers, and shoe repairers and have even cleaned laundry for the troops. The combat soldier cannot do his or her job without the Quartermaster Corps.

Today, the list of supplies that the Quartermaster Corps must obtain includes the fuel needed to run the army's vehicles. But before the age of trucks, jeeps, and aircraft, the Quartermaster Corps had to find and train horses. When horse cavalry units were no longer used, mules were still needed as pack animals as late as World War II. It was during World War II that dogs were first trained to perform various duties. For a few years, the army even tried to use camels!

The supplies have changed over the years, but the responsibilities are the same for the Quartermaster Corps. These soldiers are at work in Vietnam in 1967.

At the peak of World War II, Quartermasters were supplying more than 70,000 different items and providing more than 24 million meals each day. Many Quartermasters worked in the field. During World War II, 4,943 Quartermaster soldiers were killed.

Horses and mules

Horses and mules were the first animals used by the U.S. Army. They were used for riding and to haul water, food, ammunition, and artillery. Horses and mules also pulled wagons that removed the wounded from the battlefields. They were used from 1775 until 1957, but World War I was the last time that large numbers of horses

The mascot of the U.S. Military Academy at West Point is a mule.

and mules were used. At first, the Quartermaster Department bought the animals from private citizens. Often, they ended up with older animals that were not too healthy.

In 1908, Congress established the Remount Service. The Remount Service found the horses and then took care of them to make sure they were in good condition. Then, they trained them before sending them to their service units. During World War I, the Remount Service processed about 571,000 horses and mules. By the early 1930s, more and more armored carriers and other vehicles were being used.

A soldier leads a mule carrying radio equipment for **communications** during World War II.

In the early days of World War II, the Army had 16,800 horses and 3,500 mules available. But trucks and jeeps were becoming standard vehicles for transportation. In the end, only 49 horses were shipped overseas during the war. But in 1944 and 1945, there was a need for mules to help move troops and supplies in the mountains of northern Italy and in Asia. About 14,000 mules were used during this two-year period.

Black Jack: a special horse

Black Jack was the last horse processed by the Quartermaster Corps to the U.S. Army. He was born in 1947. The Army was no longer using horses in combat, but Black Jack took part in many ceremonies, including parades and military funerals. A horse without a rider and with the boots placed backward in the stirrups is a symbol of a fallen hero. One of Black Jack's last official duties was performed at the funeral of President John F. Kennedy, when he walked in the funeral procession. Black Jack died in 1976 at the age of 29.

Black Jack was named after World War I General John J. "Black Jack" Pershing, Supreme Commander of the American Expeditionary Force in World War I.

A soldier's best friend

Dogs were first trained and used by the U.S. Army in World War II. Shortly after the attack on Pearl Harbor in Hawaii in 1941, the American Kennel Club and a group called Dogs for Defense encouraged dog owners to give their dogs to the Quartermaster Corps for war service. More than 19,000 dogs were donated, but almost half of them were not accepted for training. Belgian sheep dogs, Doberman pinschers, collies, and giant schnauzers were used. There were even a few mutts in the service. Today, however, all army dogs are German shepherds.

Know It

During World War I, the United States borrowed dogs from the British and French armies. Many of these dogs were known as mercy dogs. They were trained to search the battlefield for wounded soldiers. Then, they would lead medics to the wounded men so they could be treated.

Prince, the dog, is receiving instructions on where to carry the message in the pack on his back.

Dogs are trained for four types of duty. Most dogs are sentry dogs. They are trained to alert their handlers if a stranger is approaching or hiding nearby. Each dog has its own way of "saying" that danger is near. For many dogs, the signal is when their hair stands up on their back. In Vietnam, a dog named Major would cross his ears when he sensed trouble. Another one, named Eric, would walk on his hind legs.

In World War II, 10,425 dogs were trained for war duty. Of those, 9,300 were trained for sentry duty. In the Korean War, about 1,500 dogs were used. In Vietnam, about 4,000 dogs were in active service. Dogs have also been used in the Persian Gulf War.

Scout, or patrol dogs have skills in addition to those needed for sentry duty. They can work in complete silence to help find **snipers.** Scout dogs also can detect the enemy waiting to **ambush** American soldiers. Messenger dogs must work with two handlers so they can deliver messages. They learn to move silently and find cover on their own while on a mission. Mine dogs are trained to find booby traps and trip wires attached to mines, or small bombs.

This is Chips, one of the best war dogs from World War II.

War dog heroes

One dog who served in World War II was given combat medals. However, it was against army policy to award medals to animals and they were taken away. In 1944 the war department changed its mind in a way. It allowed public commendations to be issued. That means an official public statement is made about the dog's bravery and courage. Later, citation certificates were given to outstanding dogs. These are still used. The citations list the dog's accomplishments.

The U.S. Army Camel Corps

In the mid-1800s, a second lieutenant suggested that camels might be useful in the deserts of the southwest United States. The hot weather and difficult terrain (land) were very hard on horses and mules. After several years of discussions, Congress finally gave some money for the project.

In June, 1855, the ship USS *Supply* set sail to get the camels. It finally landed in Egypt. Major Henry C. Wayne bought 33 camels and hired five camel handlers to return with them to the United States. After a two-month trip, they arrived in Texas in April 1856.

This painting shows members of the U.S. Camel Corps in 1857.

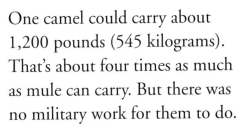

Hi Jolly memorial

Hadji Ali was a Syrian camel handler who came to the United States in 1856 with the camels purchased by the U.S. Army. When the experiment ended, he kept some camels and tried to run a freight business to move goods. The business failed, and he released his camels into the desert. When he died in 1902, he believed that a few of his camels were still roaming the desert. Soldiers had trouble pronouncing his name and called him Hi Jolly. That is the name on the monument.

One camel could carry about 1,200 pounds (545 kilograms). That's about four times as much as mule can carry. But there was no military work for them to do. Finally, in June 1857 the camels were used on an expedition to explore unknown territory between El Paso, Texas, and the Colorado River. When the expedition got lost, the camels found a river and led everyone to it. They did complete their mission and reached the Colorado River.

However, the soldiers did not like them. They thought the camels smelled bad and had bad tempers. A new commander also did not like the camels. The camels were not being used enough to make up for the cost of taking care of them. Then, the Civil War began and the experiment ended. Most of the camels were sold to zoos, circuses, and mining companies. Many of them were later turned loose and wandered through Texas, California, and Arizona for years.

Army Equipment and Vehicles

Over the years, the army has designed tanks, aircraft, and even trucks and jeeps to help them apply new warfare **tactics.** Tanks were first used on the battlefields of World War I. They were dangerous to operate and did not always work well. But by using tracks instead of wheels, the tanks could climb over and plow through the toughest combat conditions. By the end of World War I, the U.S. Army was convinced that tanks were the vehicles of the future. Here are a few army vehicles.

Know It

The term *tank* was first used to describe tracked combat vehicles during World War I. To keep the enemy from learning about their design, they were called tanks. It was thought that the enemy would think they were steel containers.

The Abrams M1 Tank

The Abrams M1 is the main battle tank of the Army and the most powerful armored fighting vehicle in the world. It weighs as much as five school buses, yet it can travel over sand dunes and deserts at 40 miles (64 kilometers) per hour. No other tank has as much firepower.

Helicopters

The AH-64 Attack Helicopters are the army's main attack helicopters. They are also called the Apache helicopters. The newest version, the AH-64D Apache Longbow, can fire missiles, rockets, and regular gun ammunition.

Deep water does not stop an M-1 Abrams tank (left). An Apache helicopter heads off on a mission (right).

The comanche does not look like other helicopters because of its **stealth** technology.

The super-quiet RAH-66 Comanche has **stealth technology.** This helps it avoid being found by enemy radar. It will soon be the army's main **surveillance** and attack helicopter. The Comanche can fly day or night and in all weather conditions. Its purpose is to locate enemy positions. Using special **infrared sensors,** the Comanche chooses the best targets. It then reports the targets to the Apache Longbow.

When it comes to **transporting** troops and equipment, the twin-engine CH-47 Chinook leads the way. This helicopter has proven to be especially valuable when operating in areas far from roads and railways.

Personal gear

Soldiers with the special operations forces are given a Ghillie Suit Accessory Kit (GSAK) to help protect them in the field. The kit contains materials to make and repair **camouflage** clothes, including sewing needles, thread, and fabric. The kits have white pants, jackets, and mittens for camouflage in snowy conditions. The kits also have camouflage clothes for soldiers in forest or desert areas.

A CH-47 Chinook prepares to land.

Heroes: Medals and Awards

When members of the U.S. Army perform their jobs to the best of their ability and under difficult conditions, they can be given medals, known officially as decorations. There are dozens of decorations. They are awarded for combat and noncombat performance of duty. Here are some of them.

The Medal of Honor is the highest medal a person can earn. It was first established by an act of Congress in 1862. Hundreds of thousands of people have served in the army since the nation was founded. Only 4,428 people have received this award. To earn it, a person must distinguish himself or herself "by gallantry at the risk of his life or her life above and beyond the call of duty while engaged in an action against an enemy of the United States."

Purple Hearts are awarded to any member of the armed forces who has been wounded or killed while participating in any action against an enemy of the United States. This award was first established by General George Washington in 1782.

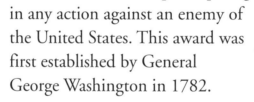

In 1985, Congress authorized a Prisoner of War (POW) Medal. The POW Medal is given to military **personnel** who have been held captive by an enemy of the United States. It was given to people who served as long ago as 1917 to honor their sacrifice and suffering on behalf of their country.

The Combat Field Medical badge was created in 1945 by the war department. It is awarded to

Medal of Honor

Purple Heart

officers and **enlisted personnel** of the medical department who "shared the same hazards and hardships of ground combat on a daily basis with the infantry soldier."

In today's army, personnel can have many types of duties to perform. Sometimes keeping the peace means not picking up a gun. In 1977, by order of President James Carter, the **Humanitarian** Service Medal was established. It is given to members of the armed forces whose performance during a humanitarian operation (not combat) is exceptional.

General Colin Powell, who became secretary of state when he retired from the army, earned many honors during his career.

Prisoner of War Medal

Humanitarian Service Medal

Fruit salad?

Fruit salad is a slang term for the numerous medals, badges, and decorations often seen grouped together on the uniforms of army officers. This nickname came about because of the many colors, shapes, and textures that are in the design of the various awards.

Glossary

active duty involved in military service full-time

allied armed forces from various countries fighting together under a single command

ambush surprise attack from a hidden position

artillery heavy guns, cannons

barracks military housing for enlisted personnel

cabinet officials selected by the president to head the departments of government.

cadets students attending military schools who are training to be officers

camouflage method of disguising soldier's location using colors and materials.

civilian a person who is not in the armed forces

commission official document giving military personnel certain rank or power

commissioned given an officer's title

communications sharing information

conventional normal, not unusual

deploy to position troops or weapons on the battlefield

draft process in which young men put their names on a list that the government can use when it needs to call them to fight a war

enlisted military personnel who have not achieved the rank of officer

formation a set pattern

front lines place where the main battle takes place

guerrilla soldiers that strike at the enemy in small bands often by surprise

humanitarian having to do with helping people by providing medical care and food, water, and other supplies

infantry soldier who fights on foot

infrared sensors instruments that detect, or find, a source of heat from a target

intelligence secret information about an enemy

mechanized using tanks, trucks and other vehicles instead of horses or mules

militia an army made up of ordinary citizens instead of regular soldiers

minority a group within a community that has a different race, religion, or national origin from most of the people in that group

personnel people who work for the armed forces or a business company

reconnaissance a mission to gather information

sniper someone who shoots from a hidden position

stealth the ability to prevent being seen by enemy radar

surveillance secretly watch something or someone

tactic plan or idea for performing a task

technology ideas and equipment that help people perform complicated tasks

transporting sending something or someone to another place

trenches long narrow holes, or ditches,

unconventional unusual

More Books to Read

Gartman, Gene. *Life in Army Basic Training.* Danbury, Conn.: Children's Press, 2000.

Hopkins, Ellen H. *The Golden Knights: The U.S. Army Parachute Team.* Mankato, Minn.: Capstone Press, 2001.

Kennedy, Robert C. *Life as an Army Demolition Expert.* Danbury, Conn.: Children's Press, 2000.

Ward, S. and Stasia Ward Kehoe. *I Live at a Military Post.* New York: Rosen Publishing Group, 1999.

Index